ELIZABETH
DOLE

PUBLIC SERVANT AND SENATOR

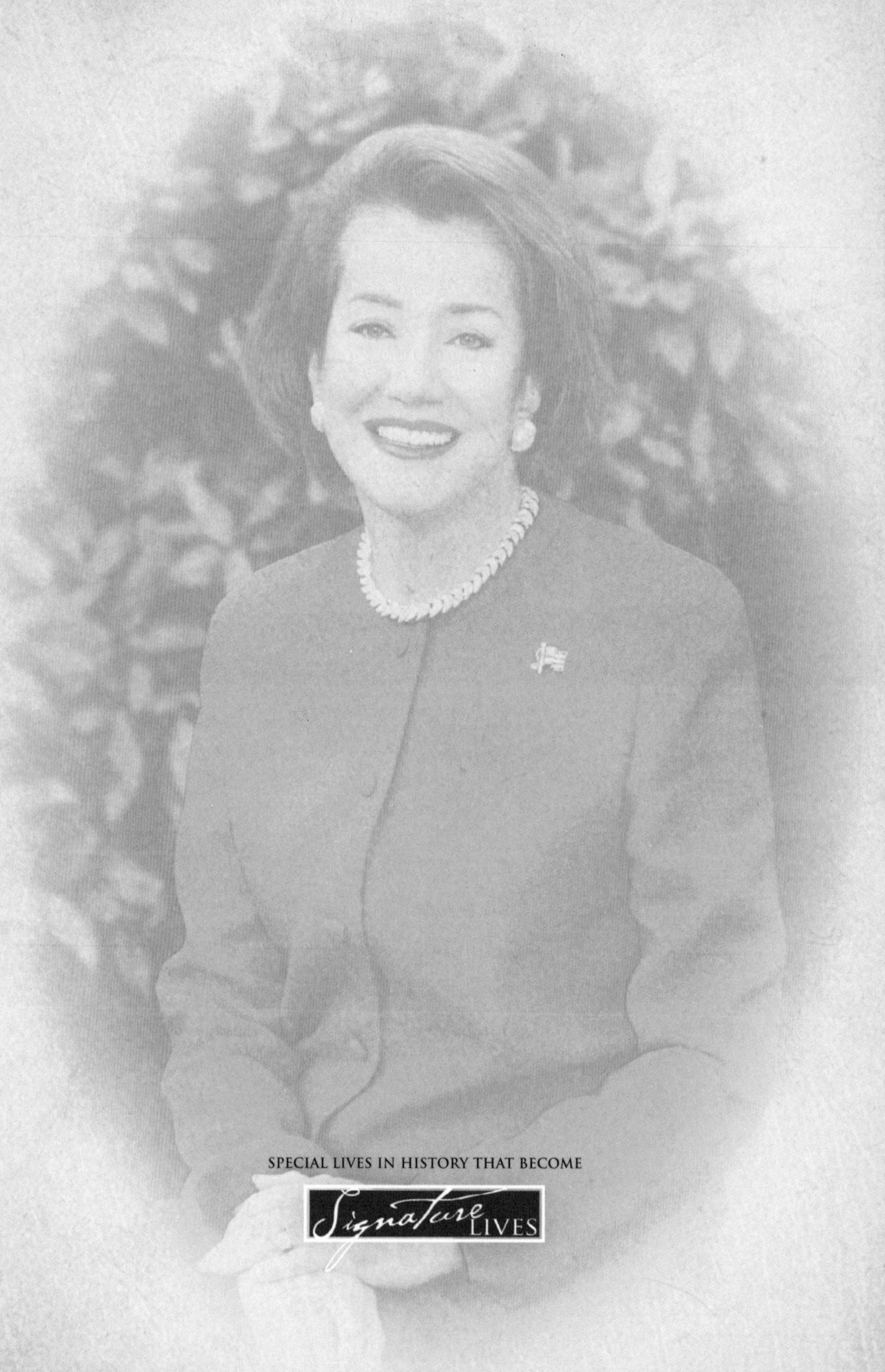
SPECIAL LIVES IN HISTORY THAT BECOME
Signature LIVES

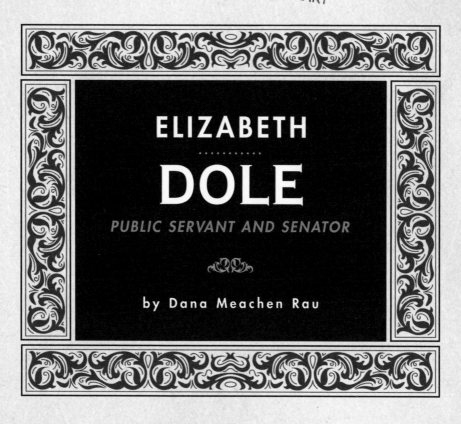

ELIZABETH
DOLE

PUBLIC SERVANT AND SENATOR

by Dana Meachen Rau

Content Adviser: Andrew J. Taylor, Ph.D.,
Chair, Department of Political Science,
North Carolina State University

Reading Adviser: Rosemary G. Palmer, Ph.D.,
Department of Literacy, College of Education,
Boise State University

Compass Point Books ✦ Minneapolis, Minnesota

Compass Point Books
3109 West 50th Street, #115
Minneapolis, MN 55410

Visit Compass Point Books on the Internet at *www.compasspointbooks.com*
or e-mail your request to *custserv@compasspointbooks.com*

Editors: Sue Vander Hooke and Mari Bolte
Page Production: Bobbie Nuytten
Photo Researchers: Marcie C. Spence and Svetlana Zhurkin
Cartographer: XNR Productions, Inc.
Library Consultant: Kathleen Baxter

Art Director: Jaime Martens
Creative Director: Keith Griffin
Editorial Director: Nick Healy
Managing Editor: Catherine Neitge

Library of Congress Cataloging-in-Publication Data
Rau, Dana Meachen, 1971–
    Elizabeth Dole : public servant and senator / by Dana Meachen Rau.
       p. cm.—(Signature lives)
    Includes bibliographical references and index.
    ISBN 978-0-7565-1583-6 (library binding)
    ISBN 0-7565-1583-1 (library binding)
    1. Dole, Elizabeth —-Juvenile literature. 2. Women cabinet officers—
United States—Biography—Juvenile literature. 3. Cabinet officers—
United States—Biography—Juvenile literature. 4. American Red Cross—
Biography—Juvenile literature. 5. Women legislators—United States—
Biography—Juvenile literature. 6. Legislators—United—Biography—
Juvenile literature. 7. United States. Congress. Senate—Biography—
Juvenile literature.   I. Title. II. Series.
E840.8.D63R38 2006
973.929092—dc22
    [B]   2005025095

Signature Lives

MODERN AMERICA

Life in the United States since the late 19th century has undergone incredible changes. Advancements in technology and in society itself have transformed the lives of Americans. As they adjusted to this modern era, people cast aside old ways and embraced new ideas. The once silenced members of society—women, minorities, and young people—made their voices heard. Modern Americans survived wars, economic depression, protests, and scandals to emerge strong and ready to face whatever the future holds.

Elizabeth Dole

Table of Contents

1 No Women Allowed

❦

Elizabeth Hanford hurried down the sidewalk in Washington, D.C. It was the early 1970s, and the capital of the United States was filled with people making important decisions about America's future. The president in the White House, the representatives and senators in the Capitol, and many men and women working in other government offices held daily meetings to propose, discuss, and decide new laws. Elizabeth Hanford worked for the Office of Consumer Affairs. She and the people of her office watched out for the public by making sure the goods they bought were safe and the labels were factual and honest.

Most of the people working in powerful government positions were men. Elizabeth was one of the few

Elizabeth Hanford Dole has held two Cabinet posts, worked for six presidents, and served as a U.S. senator.

women among them, but she was used to that. And she never saw being a woman as something that kept her back. At Harvard Law School, she had been one of just 24 women in a class of more than 550, but she was smart and talented and kept up with her male-dominated class. After getting her law degree, Elizabeth moved to Washington, D.C.

Being the only woman in the Harvard International Law Club prepared Elizabeth for a career in male-dominated politics.

Now Elizabeth was on her way to a meeting with lawyers from Cleveland, Ohio. She had spent the entire weekend preparing for this day. Preparation, she felt, was the most important thing you could do before a presentation. It showed that you respected your audience and had taken the time to learn all the

issues. She tried to get to know as much as she could about the people she would be talking with.

When Elizabeth reached the Metropolitan Club, she told the doorman that she was from the White House and was there for a meeting. But he refused to let her in. "I don't care if you're Queen Elizabeth," he said. "You can't go in, this club is for men only."

When one of the men she was to meet arrived, he apologized. He said that when he had set up the meeting, he didn't know this social club, which had been established during the Civil War, excluded women. Elizabeth offered to go back to the Office of Consumer Affairs and get a man to take her place. Or, she suggested, they could reschedule the meeting at a different place so she could attend. But the Ohio lawyers held the meeting without her, and she went back to her office.

Elizabeth was upset. She liked to be in control, and, as a manager

The Metropolitan Club has been called the grandest of Washington, D.C.'s private clubs. Located near the White House, it is known as a place where politicians and other leaders can escape from the public. Athletic facilities, entertainment, dining, and overnight amenities are available for members' use. The dress code inside the club is formal, and no cell phones or other communication devices are allowed. Potential members must be nominated and accepted by existing members. Since Elizabeth's failed meeting, the club has started to admit women, although the facilities available to women are still not equal to those available to the men.

and planner, she didn't like surprises. That closed door at the Metropolitan Club was beyond her control, but she didn't let that setback stop her. Instead, she strengthened her resolve to show those men, and America, that women could hold powerful positions. "Indeed, there were many times early in my career," she said, "when I looked around the meeting table and realized that I was the only woman there." She worked hard to prove that women were equal to men in the workplace.

Throughout her active life, Elizabeth Hanford Dole has risen to high positions within the U.S. government and used her powerful positions to help others. She has devoted herself to public service, working to make conditions at job sites safer, to upgrade the skills of American workers, and to make roads safe. When natural disasters and war have devastated people's lives and homes, Elizabeth Dole has been there to help.

In 2003, Dole began serving as U.S. senator from her home state of North Carolina. She often shares her enthusiasm for public service with others:

> *I tell youthful audiences they can find no higher calling in life than that of public service. They may not get rich, but they'll enrich the lives of countless others. … Because of them, the world is a little better.*

Elizabeth Hanford Dole has dedicated her life to trying to make her country and the world a better place for all people. ❧

Elizabeth Dole (third from left in the back row) was one of the 14 women senators in 2003.

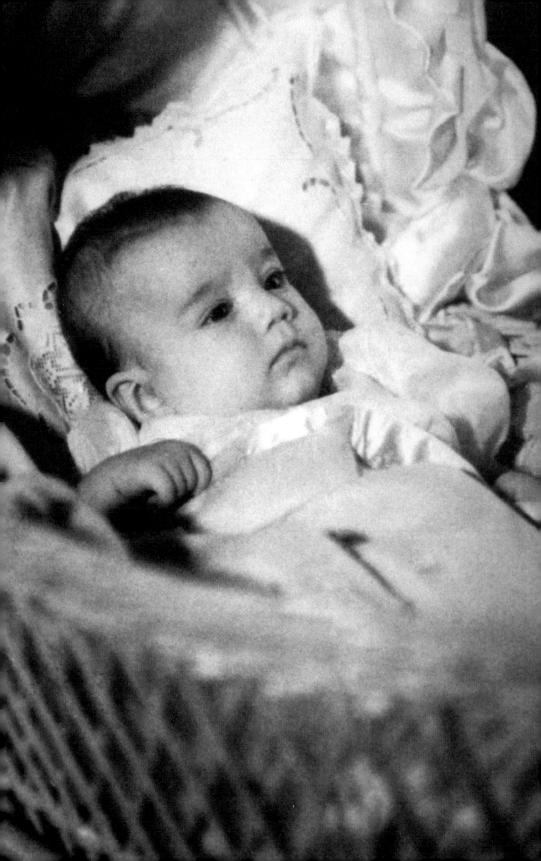

2 MOST LIKELY TO SUCCEED

❦

Elizabeth Hanford Dole's life began on July 29, 1936, in the small town of Salisbury, North Carolina. Her parents, John and Mary Hanford, couldn't decide what to name her. John wanted to call her Mary, but the proud new mother had other ideas. She hoped to name the baby Elizabeth Alexander, after her grandmother. Finally, they reached a compromise and named their daughter Mary Elizabeth Alexander Hanford. Everyone ended up calling her Elizabeth, or "Liddy," as she called herself when she turned 2.

Salisbury was a perfect place for little Elizabeth to spread her wings. Her family had deep roots in this town where Mary Hanford's Scotch-Irish ancestors settled in the 1700s before the Revolutionary War. John Hanford's family came to Salisbury at the turn of the

Although her family called her "Liddy," Elizabeth prefers her given name to be used in public.

20th century and started a flower business that John now owned. Like many other small Southern towns, neighbors were friendly and proper. Acts of kindness and faith in God were central to everyday life.

The Hanford home was both traditional and formal. Elizabeth has fond memories of her childhood in the house on South Fulton Street that she shared with her parents and brother John, who was 13 years older than Elizabeth. She always looked up to her brother John. "He has been absolutely on a pedestal, and he still is," she says of him. While John

Even as a child, young Elizabeth was full of ideas.

was off with the older boys, she often entertained herself by curling up in the nooks and crannies of the house to read books. When John spent time with Elizabeth, he noticed all the ideas that were swimming around in her head. "Even as a little tiny tyke," he said, "she always had something cooking."

Elizabeth's father was a strict but loving parent. He was a hard worker who disciplined his children when he was home. Elizabeth greatly admired her mother, who was devoted to her husband, her children, and her church. Into adulthood, Elizabeth stayed close to her mother, who lived to be more than 100 years old.

The family business made the Hanfords wealthy, and they always had what they needed. During the summers, Elizabeth attended camp or stayed at the family cabin outside Salisbury. She had many interests, including ballet, horseback riding, and piano, and she often performed in piano recitals.

Music was important to the Hanfords. Elizabeth's father often dressed up in his shiny uniform to conduct the Salisbury municipal band. When Elizabeth's mother was younger, she had planned to attend

Young Elizabeth Hanford loved pets. During her youth, she had a pet cat named Beauty and a Chihuahua named Penny. She was crushed when they died, and she buried them under the magnolia tree in the backyard of her house on Fulton Street. As an adult, she had two miniature schnauzers named Leader and Leader II.

The Juilliard School

the Juilliard School in New York to become a music instructor. But when she met John Hanford, she set aside her plans and turned her attention to her family. Whenever she could, she brought music into the lives of her family members.

Elizabeth's grandparents, Pop and Mom Cathey, as she called them, lived on the same street as the Hanfords. On Sundays, Elizabeth loved to spend time with Mom Cathey. Neighbors of all ages and other family members would gather to eat cookies and drink lemonade in Mom Cathey's living room, where she often told them Bible stories.

While Elizabeth's childhood was going along peacefully in Salisbury, soldiers were fighting in World War II in Europe and Asia. Even though the battlefields were on the other side of the Atlantic

Ocean, the war still affected American families, and it affected the Hanfords. Elizabeth's brother served in the U.S. Navy aboard the USS *Saratoga*. The Hanfords worried about him much of the time.

The Allies, including the United States, were fighting against the Germans and their brutal dictator, Adolf Hitler. Elizabeth was only 3 when the war in Europe started, so she was too young to understand the reasons for the war, but she did learn from it. "I found it a continuing lesson in sensitivity to the feelings of others," she said. As young as she was, she did what she could to help. Elizabeth and some other girls organized a recycling drive in their neighborhood to help the troops overseas. The older girls crocheted squares to make blankets for the troops. In 1945, when Elizabeth was 9 years old, John finally came home safely on survivor's leave after his ship was hit by Japanese bombers. He brought Elizabeth home a little uniform of her own.

"My mother and dad were both people who believed in hard work and strong values," Elizabeth said.

World War II (1939-1945) involved many nations of the world. It began when Germany invaded Poland, an attempt by Adolf Hitler, dictator of Germany, to conquer all of Europe. The United States joined with other nations to fight him in 1941. More than 15 million American men and almost 350,000 women served in the military then. Factories in America built tanks, aircraft, ships, weapons, and equipment for the war. While the men were away fighting, many women worked in these factories.

The USS Saratoga, *the aircraft carrier on which Elizabeth's brother served, transported Navy veterans home after the Japanese surrendered in 1945.*

And Elizabeth inherited these characteristics of her parents. Elizabeth remembers her mother saying, "If it's worth doing, it's worth giving it your all, giving it your very best effort." At Boyden High School in Salisbury, she was a straight-A student. In her free time, she wrote essays and entered them in contests. When she ran for class president and lost, she didn't let that stop her from running for other offices. She loved being a part of student government. The school was used to male leadership and wasn't ready for a female president, she thought. She never lost her confidence, and later she was voted Most Likely to Succeed.

Elizabeth always strived to please her teachers and her family. But when it came to college, Elizabeth thought more about her own interests and needs. In the mid-1950s, most women did not work outside the home. Girls were taught how to cook and sew and manage a house for a husband and family. But Elizabeth did not want to be a homemaker. She wanted a career and decided to apply to Duke University in Durham, North Carolina. Her brother had attended Duke, and she wanted to follow in his footsteps.

Elizabeth's mother urged her to focus her studies on home economics and take classes in cooking and sewing. Elizabeth, however, had her own ideas, as she always had. Mary Hanford tried to steer her to a life at home, but she knew her daughter was very independent. In a family photo album, next to a picture of 1-year-old Elizabeth, Mary had written even then, "She is very willful and insists on having her own way." Elizabeth said that Mary had also raised her to work hard:

> *... encouraging me to really put an effort into what I was doing, and I think also a sense of mission that is important in life to try to make a difference, a positive difference for others.*

Elizabeth didn't major in home economics at Duke. Instead, pulled by her desire to learn more about her country, she chose political science. ℘

Chapter

3 A WOMAN AMONG MEN

❧⟨✕⟩☙

In the fall of 1954, Elizabeth Hanford left Salisbury and went to Durham, North Carolina, to attend Duke University. Since the late 1800s, the university had offered quality education to both men and women. In the 1950s, men and women attended classes together, but they lived on separate campuses—women on the East Campus and men on the West Campus.

As she had through grade school and high school, Elizabeth excelled in her studies. She also learned the importance of having good public speaking skills. "One of the first lessons I learned at Duke," she said, "is that the ability to speak clearly and persuasively is essential to achieving your goals." Weekends were spent going out and dancing with friends or attending fancier school-sponsored events. Outside of class,

Duke University was founded in 1838, when Methodist and Quaker families hired the first full-time teacher for their school in Durham.

she worked on the staff for the *Chanticleer*, the university's yearbook, and sang in the choir and in a women's singing group called a glee club. She joined the sorority Delta Delta Delta, which was known for its community service projects.

Throughout her life, Elizabeth always looked to successful women as role models. Her first examples were her mother and grandmother. Now, beyond the borders of her hometown, she found other admirable women to learn from. Roberta Florence Brinkley became one of her role models at Duke. An English professor and dean, or head, of the women's campus, Brinkley opened up her home to students on Sunday afternoons. Just like her Sundays with Mom Cathey, Elizabeth now went for tea at Brinkley's home, where she listened to this successful woman and learned everything she could from her. Brinkley inspired Elizabeth and her other students to think for themselves.

When Elizabeth was a senior, she was elected president of the Women's Student Government Association.

Roberta Florence Brinkley was the dean of the Women's College at Duke University from 1947 to 1962.

At the end of the year, the *Chronicle,* the campus newspaper, praised her work:

> *Women's Student Government Association itself was perhaps the pinnacle of campus organizations this year because of Miss Hanford's leadership. While demanding the hard work and efficiency from her subordinates that are necessary for such accomplishments, Miss Hanford maintained a sense of responsibility to those who elected her, a quality which forceful leaders often forget.*

For her academic achievement, Elizabeth was accepted as a member of Phi Beta Kappa, an academic honor society. She was also accepted as a member of the White Duchy, another honor society that recognizes strong female leaders. The other women seniors at Duke chose her that year to be their May Queen. She had given much to the Duke community, and the *Chronicle* named her Leader of the Year.

Some famous women have graduated from Duke University. Juanita Kreps graduated in 1948, and in 1977 she became the first woman to serve as U.S. Secretary of Commerce. Eleanor Smeal, who graduated in 1961, was involved in women's political issues and became the president of the National Organization for Women (NOW). Annabeth Gish, a 1993 graduate, became an actress and starred in many television dramas. Alana Beard was a high-scoring basketball star at Duke and, after graduating in 2004, went on to play for the Women's National Basketball Association.

Elizabeth graduated from Duke on June 2, 1958. Out of 37 political science majors, she was the only one with high enough grades to graduate with honors. Now she had to decide what direction to take. She could go back to Salisbury to work in the family flower business or get married, as many of her friends were doing. In fact, the summer after she graduated, Elizabeth was a bridesmaid in eight friends' weddings. She was dating a man from a nearby college, and her parents would have been pleased if she had decided to get married.

But Elizabeth was not ready to settle down. With a good education and the world before her, she decided she could do anything she wanted. Although most women still held to the traditional role of wives and mothers, many were thinking about education and careers. The world's view of women was changing, and their place in society and the workplace was becoming more important. On March 7, 1960, *Newsweek* magazine reported:

> *Who could ask for anything more? The educated American woman has her brains, her good looks, her car, her freedom ... freedom to choose a straight-from-Paris dress (original or copy), or to attend a class in ceramics or calculus; freedom to determine the timing of her next baby or who shall be next President of the United States.*

But Elizabeth was not sure what she wanted to do next. Brinkley suggested that she go to Oxford University in England. That certainly fit her curious and adventurous personality and her desire to learn and discover new things about herself and the world. In the summer of 1959, Elizabeth left North Carolina

Oxford University was a place of education as early as 1096. Women were not allowed entry until 1920.

and went to Oxford, England, where she took classes in English history and government at the university. When she wasn't attending classes, she explored England. She even found time to travel to the Soviet Union, which made her parents unhappy. The United States and the Soviet Union were locked in the Cold War—a conflict that did not result in actual war but was a time of constant tension over the use of nuclear weapons—and the Hanfords feared for Elizabeth's safety. Elizabeth, however, was not afraid, and she thoroughly enjoyed her adventure.

When Elizabeth returned to the United States, she decided to live in Massachusetts. The summer before she went to England, she had worked at the law library at Harvard University in Cambridge, Massachusetts. She liked the school, and she liked Cambridge, so in September 1959, she enrolled in a program that combined studies in government and teaching. For her teaching credential, she served as a student teacher at a high school in Melrose, Massachusetts. History was an exciting subject to her, and she tried to share that enthusiasm. She invited guest speakers to the classroom who could make history come alive for her students. She hoped that events and people in the past were not just words on a written page or part of a lecture. She wanted them to be real and interesting.

When Elizabeth graduated from the year-long program, she was still restless. Though she had

B. Everett Jordan served as U.S. senator from 1958 to 1973.

enjoyed her teaching experience, she found she was drawn more to government. In the summer of 1960, she moved to Washington, D.C., where she worked in the office of North Carolina's Democratic Senator B. Everett Jordan. That summer, she also joined the presidential campaign of Democrat John F. Kennedy and his running mate, Lyndon B. Johnson. Joining Johnson on a train tour of the South, she was exposed for the first time to campaigning. After Kennedy and

Johnson won the election, Elizabeth moved on to New York City, where she worked at the United Nations as a tour guide and intern, a trainee who works at a low-level job to gain practical experience.

Elizabeth met many people at her job. One of them was Margaret Chase Smith, a senator from Maine, who encouraged her to get a law degree. She said it could only help her in whatever career path she chose.

Margaret Chase Smith, who served in both the House and the Senate is known as one of the most successful politicians in Maine history.

MARY ELIZABETH HANFORD
B.A. Duke '58; M.A. Harvard '6(
712 So. Fulton St., Salisbury, N.C
Marshall, B. & B., I.L.C., S.C.
RICHARD ANTHONY HAN
B.A. Boston College '62
1084 Adams St., Dorchester, N
Freund, I.L.C., Record, S. Bar,
JEROME DANIEL HANSCU
B.S. Marquette Univ. '62
2718 Central Ave., Cheyenne, '
Warren B & B Dorm C S

Elizabeth's 1964 Harvard Law School yearbook picture

When Elizabeth broke the news to her parents, her mother was upset. Why didn't her daughter want to be a wife and mother? Mary Hanford had always lived in Salisbury and enjoyed being a homemaker, and she couldn't understand why Elizabeth didn't want that kind of future. Elizabeth tried to explain. She wanted to get married someday and settle down with a husband, but not right now. She had too many plans—the most important of which was to have a career.

In 1962, Elizabeth entered Harvard Law School, confident of her decision. She was encouraged when her parents finally accepted the fact that their daughter was pursuing a career. Even Elizabeth, who always enjoyed a challenge, found her time at Harvard to be one of the hardest periods of her life. The course work was difficult and time-consuming.

Harvard Law School students were mostly men—

In 1879, Harvard University established a women's college, later called Radcliffe. Harvard professors taught the women Harvard courses, but the students were not considered Harvard students. During World War II, women were finally allowed to attend Harvard. This was mostly for convenience, since many students were overseas and it was easier to have the remaining students together. Women were allowed to attend the medical and law schools in 1945 and 1950. In 1970 Harvard and Radcliffe were made coeducational, and in 1999 the schools merged. Harvard became responsible for all undergraduate students, while Radcliffe's focus was changed to postgraduate research.

out of a class of more than 550 students, only 24 were women. Some male students didn't like having women attend Harvard, and they accused Elizabeth of taking up a spot that could have been for a man. Some of the professors were even impolite. In one of her classes, the few women there were only allowed to speak on what the professor called "ladies day." Then they could only read a poem they had composed. Women were not respected for their hard work. One classmate, Elizabeth Holtzman, who later became a member of Congress and a district attorney in New York, remembers the event. "It did succeed in humiliating us," she said. "We didn't have women's consciousness in those days. Everybody swallowed it."

If her time at Harvard could be considered a test, then Elizabeth passed it. She studied hard, and graduated in 1965. She learned to be tough, and she never gave up the battle. She proved that she was as

A group photo shows how outnumbered the women were at Harvard. Elizabeth is front and center.

capable as any man at Harvard Law School.

Now Elizabeth finally had to decide what direction she wanted for her life. She didn't want to work for a big law firm, and besides, very few of them were hiring women. Without a job in mind, she moved to Washington, D.C., the center of U.S. government and a place where she could pursue her interest in public service. Somehow, Elizabeth Hanford wanted to make a difference in the world. 🕊

Chapter
4 FINDING HER WAY IN WASHINGTON, D.C.

❧

When she arrived in Washington, D.C., in 1966, Elizabeth Hanford was immediately interested in a job opening at the U.S. Department of Health, Education, and Welfare. The department hired her and assigned her the task of organizing a national meeting on the education of deaf people. She enthusiastically put her organizational skills to work and created a very successful conference.

Although she liked her job, she really wanted to use her law degree and start practicing law. But she needed a place to sharpen her courtroom skills. Just to watch and learn, Elizabeth would often attend night court and observe the law in action. Typically, some of the most serious cases involving robberies, drugs, and guns were heard at night. One evening, a

Washington, D.C., has been the capital city of the United States since 1800, when the capital was moved there from Philadelphia, Pennsylvania. The initials "D.C." stand for District of Columbia, which is a district and not a state. All branches of the U.S. government are centered there—the executive branch, headed by the president; the legislative branch, made up of the Senate and House of Representatives; and the judicial branch—made up of the justices of the Supreme Court—which oversees the court system.

judge needed a lawyer right away. A man accused of upsetting a lion at the Washington National Zoo didn't have a lawyer to defend him. When the judge found out that a lawyer—Elizabeth Hanford—was in the courtroom, he appointed her to defend the man. She won the case.

Helping people who couldn't afford a lawyer appealed to Elizabeth. She decided to spend a year as a public defender. It was a volunteer job, so she received no pay, but she got a lot of experience in a short time.

In 1968, she found another job, this time with President Lyndon B. Johnson's Committee on Consumer Interests. Johnson had become president in 1963 when John F. Kennedy was assassinated. He was elected for a full term in 1964. This committee was part of Johnson's Great Society program, one of many programs he had started in hopes of changing America for the better. The job of the committee members was to protect customers. They made rules and regulations to ensure that goods and services consumers pur-

President Lyndon B. Johnson hoped to "build a great society, a place where the meaning of man's life matches the marvels of man's labor."

chased were safe and that manufacturers were fair and honest.

In order for consumers to make wise choices, Hanford said, they must have all the important information. One focus of her work was food labeling. She and her co-workers made sure food labels were truthful and that all the ingredients were listed. Grocery items had to have freshness dates, and nutritionists were hired to study foods, such as

Lyndon B. Johnson's
Great Society programs
were created to improve
life in America. They
aimed to help the poor
by cutting taxes and
building low-income
housing in cities. They
helped education by
giving more government
money to schools
and by starting the
National Foundation
on the Arts and
Humanities for
artists and musicians.
Johnson helped end
discrimination with
the passage of the
Civil Rights Act and
Immigration Act.
Other programs helped
the environment by
setting aside forest lands
and making stricter
rules for water and air
quality. For consumers,
programs mandated
truth in packaging
labels as well as safer
highways and other
forms of transportation.

hot dogs, to make sure manufacturers didn't add a lot of unhealthy ingredients to them. The committee made sure food was not poorly made and that people didn't have to pay too much for it. Overall, the committee tried to find ways to make both the consumers and the manufacturers happy, which was sometimes a challenge.

In 1969, Richard M. Nixon became the new president of the United States. Sometimes when a president takes office, committees change or end. Nixon, however, felt it was important to protect consumers, and he kept Hanford's committee. But the name was changed to the White House Office of Consumer Affairs. Hanford also changed. She had grown up as a member of the Democratic Party, but now under Nixon, she became an independent.

Hanford's boss, Virginia Knauer, was a dynamic woman who had recognized Elizabeth's potential. She chose her to be her deputy.

Like many other role models in Hanford's life, Knauer taught her a lot. Hanford described Knauer as a mentor and a mother.

Knauer involved Hanford in many meetings and projects to give her as much experience as she could. Hanford remembered:

Virginia gave me every opportunity. She wanted to see me learn, and grow. ... She sent me to testify before Congress. I had my first press conference when I was with her. I got to meet with business groups. For five years, she was such a giving person, wanting me to have every opportunity.

Like Elizabeth, President Nixon was an alumni of Duke University, where he received his law degree.

Hanford's first public speech was at a seminar for women in the state of Kansas. After her speech, reporters crowded outside to ask her questions. She was surprised and pleased that people were interested in what she had to say.

Even though she had an important government position, Elizabeth still had to battle the widespread idea that women should not be in decision-making

Virginia Knauer stressed the importance of women in government service.

positions. She later said:

> [E]ven as a fairly high-ranking woman in the Nixon Administration, I still encountered lingering resentment among those who saw women only as envelope stuffers. Oh, sure, we could type position papers, but having those papers ever reflect our own positions as candidates and office holders was the sort of utopian vision best left to a party platform.

Hanford wasn't the only one battling for equality for women. Throughout the United States, women

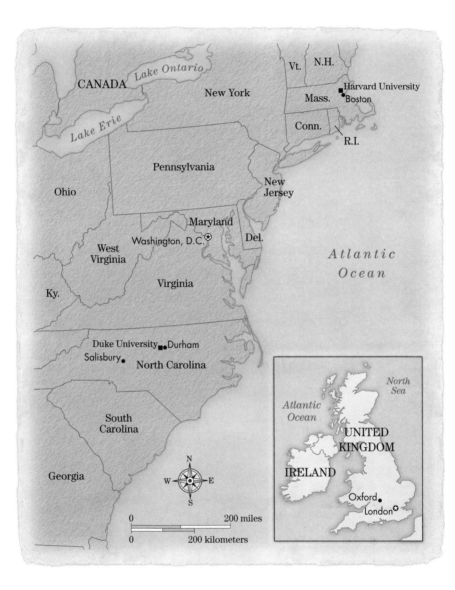

Hanford's interests led her to pursue educational and career paths far from home.

were questioning the roles that had defined them for so long. The women's movement had begun in the mid-1800s, when women began speaking out for more rights. They wanted to be able to own land, and they did not want to be considered their husbands' property. They also wanted to be allowed to vote. In 1920, women won the right to vote and help decide who their leaders in government would be. In the 1960s, women began to ask questions again. There were more women in the workforce during that time than ever before, yet they were still not paid the same wages as men (and still aren't today).

Women started to band together. Some wrote about women's rights. Others organized political groups, such as the National Organization for Women (NOW). Many more did what they could to fight for equality under the law. Their battles paid off, and more women starting going to college and earning degrees. They gained more power in employment

Founded in 1966, the National Organization for Women is the largest organization of feminist activists in the United States. It has 500,000 members and 550 chapters in all 50 states.

with the passage of equal pay laws and entered the fields of medicine and law, which had been dominated by men. They gained some power in government by running for public offices and getting jobs in government. Hanford was one of the women who was a role model for others at the time. She was proof that it was possible to be a woman and still be able to hold a position of political leadership.

Hanford had a powerful career, but she still respected women who chose to remain in a more traditional role. "Diversity is the hallmark of the modern American woman," she said, adding:

> *We wear the robes of a judge, the face mask of a surgeon, the pinstripes of a banker. We teach on campuses, peer through lab microscopes, design buildings and run businesses. Some of us write the laws that other women enforce. Some build rockets for others to ride into space. The most energetic of all run a home and raise a family. No role is superior to another.*

In 1972, Knauer and Hanford had a meeting with a senator to discuss consumer issues. He was Robert "Bob" Dole, Republican senator from Kansas and national chairman of the Republican Party. Hanford liked his honesty and sense of humor. They often saw each other at government functions, and they sometimes talked on the phone. Dole eventually asked Hanford to go to dinner with him. They had a lot in common—they were both lawyers, both from small towns, and both had government careers. Hanford admired Dole's strength and courage. He had served in World War II and returned with an injury to his arm that would leave it unusable for the rest of his life.

After several years, Elizabeth Hanford and Bob Dole were married on December 6, 1975. Elizabeth was 39 years old, and Bob was 52. He had been married before and had a daughter, Robin, but this was the first marriage for Elizabeth. The small, private wedding ceremony was held at the Washington National Cathedral's Bethlehem Chapel in Washington, D.C.

Bob did not rehearse his vows, since he had a lot of experience giving speeches without practicing. But Elizabeth pored over her notes outside the church before the ceremony. She wanted to make sure her vows were perfect, just as she would for every speech she would give in her career.

Elizabeth's parents were pleased that their

When they were married, Bob promised Elizabeth that life would never be dull. He was right.

daughter had finally married. But Bob and Elizabeth's marriage was far from the traditional model set by her parents. The Doles lived in an apartment in Washington, D.C., and their careers kept them busy and often on the road. Bob admired Elizabeth's drive and independence and considered their marriage "a lifelong partnership of equals." ᧞

5 ON THE CAMPAIGN TRAIL

∽∾∽

When Elizabeth Dole got married, she was already serving a seven-year appointment by President Nixon to the Federal Trade Commission. The purpose of the FTC is to protect people from unfair businesses and to write rules for entire industries. She helped protect the elderly who were often victims of poor care in nursing homes. She also helped women know their rights in handling their money. Again, she was protecting people's rights to be treated fairly.

When Nixon was forced to resign on August 8, 1974, because of the Watergate scandal, Vice President Gerald R. Ford became president of the United States. Elizabeth Dole continued her work for the FTC under his presidency. In 1976, Ford decided to run for a full term as president, and he chose Bob

Gerald Ford (left) knew that Bob Dole had the experience to be his vice president.

Betty Ford (left) and Elizabeth Dole both campaigned hard for their husbands in the 1976 race.

Dole as his running mate.

The Doles had been married less than a year, and Elizabeth had to make a decision. Although she had always been focused on her career, she wanted to support her new husband in his bid for vice president. In 1976, she resigned from the FTC to campaign with her husband.

Even so, she would not be a typical politician's wife. Many candidates' wives accompanied their husbands on a campaign but left the political issues alone. Elizabeth had a different view. She said:

> [A]s an independent career woman, and
> an FTC commissioner with ten years of
> government experience, I wasn't going

to spend the whole campaign answering reporters' questions with a demure 'I don't do issues.' I did do issues. Six days a week.

Ford and Dole did not win the election. Bob Dole went back to serving as senator from Kansas. Elizabeth returned to the FTC to work under the new president—Democrat Jimmy Carter.

But Bob Dole still had ambitions to hold a higher public office. In 1979, he decided to run for president. Again, Elizabeth left her job at the FTC to campaign with her husband. Some people criticized her for doing so, but she saw the campaign as a chance to give speeches and travel throughout the United States to talk to voters about their hopes for America.

Bob did not receive the Republican presidential nomination. The party instead chose Ronald Reagan, the former governor of California and movie actor. Elizabeth Dole wanted a Republican for president, so she campaigned for Reagan, giving speeches on his behalf. Reagan won the presidential election, defeating President Carter.

Reagan appreciated Elizabeth Dole's work, and in 1980, he asked her to become head of the White House Office of Public Liaison. This office was designed to keep the White House in touch with everyday people. It was Elizabeth's job to encourage the public to support Reagan's plans and programs.

Ronald Reagan is flanked by Elizabeth and Bob Dole at a White House luncheon after his election. Joining them was White House Chief of Staff, James Baker (right) and Michael Deaver.

People and groups that were working for change in the government could contact her, and she would present their ideas and opinions to the president.

Elizabeth had reached another milestone in her career—she was now working closely with the president. Yet she felt something was missing. She said:

> I began to realize that my career had become so dominant and so all-consuming and that this was not totally satisfying. I had a beautiful marriage. I loved what I was doing, and yet I'd gotten my priorities out of order.

She was working seven days a week and ignoring some important things in her life. So she turned to her church. Religion had been an important part of her childhood, when she listened to Bible stories with her grandmother and attended services with her family every Sunday at a Methodist church. Now she began attending the Foundry Methodist Church in Washington, D.C. On Monday evenings, she met with nine people from her church, and they discussed their faith and how God was working in their everyday lives. Elizabeth, who often hid her feelings behind practiced speeches, shared her thoughts with this group and told of her renewed faith. She began reading the Bible every day and set aside Sundays for worship and time with her husband.

Elizabeth also discovered that President Reagan depended on his faith in his political life. She often spoke of how she sat alone with the president before a speech and asked him how he was able to be so kind and polite even though he held the problems of the world on his shoulders. When he was faced with problems as governor of California, he said, he often looked behind him for someone else to pass the crisis on to. Then he realized that instead of looking back, he should be looking up and seeking God's help. Elizabeth kept his words in mind as she climbed the ladder of her career. ❧

6 SAFETY FIRST

❦

On February 7, 1983, President Reagan made Elizabeth Dole one of his closest advisers. She became the secretary of transportation—the only female member of his Cabinet and the first woman to ever hold that position.

Being the only woman among men was a challenge Dole had already faced in her career. But being the secretary of transportation was a special challenge. She hadn't really thought of how few women were in the transportation industry until she started work there. So she tried to increase the number of women by creating women's programs and hiring many women to help run her department, which was in charge of U.S. trains, planes, ships, cars, trucks, and buses. Today she still sees the benefits of

Elizabeth Dole, the first female secretary of transportation, was sworn in by Sandra Day O'Connor (far right), the first female Supreme Court justice. Dole's mother held the Bible.

these programs. She said:

> *Every now and then I'm going through an airport and ... a woman will come running after me saying 'Miss Dole, Miss Dole, I just wanted to tell you I was a part of your women's program at the Department of Transportation and I'm now the manager of this airport.' And that warms your heart, to be able to help some people along the way.*

At the Department of Transportation, one of her chief concerns was safety, an issue that some past officeholders had avoided. But the Doles felt nothing was more important.

The official mission of the U.S. Department of Transportation is to "serve the United States by ensuring a fast, safe, efficient, accessible and convenient transportation system that meets our vital national interests and enhances the quality of life of the American people, today and into the future."

I remember my husband and I having a real talk about what could you do that could really make a difference? And both of us felt, it's the safety issues and the traveling public. ... Where could you make a greater difference than in saving lives and protecting people against these crippling, disabling injuries?

The country's roads were still the scene of many crashes. Dole wanted people to be as safe as

possible, even if they were involved in a crash. She announced that all cars would have to have automatic seat belts or air bags by 1989. Automakers were not happy. Air bags—the inflated bags that burst out of the steering wheel or dashboard to cushion front-seat drivers in a crash—were expensive to make and install. But Dole insisted that people be safe. In order to help automakers, she said that if enough states passed seatbelt laws, then air bags would not be required. Those states had to represent at least two-thirds of the population of the United States.

New York was the first state to pass a seat belt

Bob Dole supported his wife's career as the secretary of transportation.

Airbags were not standard equipment in vehicles until 1988, and were not mandatory until 1998.

law, in 1984. Finally, enough states passed laws requiring the driver, passengers in the front seat, and children under 10 to wear a seat belt. But because Dole got her seat belt laws, she would not get the air bag requirement she also wanted.

Drunk driving was also a problem that Dole was concerned with. Every year many people died in crashes that involved someone who had been drinking. One way to lower that number, Dole thought, was to raise the legal drinking age from 18 to 21. Dole announced that any state that did not raise its drinking age would not receive as much government money to keep up its highways. The states did not want to lose these funds, and soon, all 50 states had a legal drinking age of 21.

One of her major contributions to highway safety was adding a third brake light to cars. There were already two brake lights on cars, one on each side of the back that lit up when the driver pressed the brake pedal. Dole felt a third brake light—near the base or slightly below the middle of the back windshield—would make it clearer to drivers that the car in front of them was slowing down or stopping. Many accidents were caused by one car crashing into another one from behind. The roads would be safer for all drivers, she thought. The new brake light was nicknamed "The Dole Light."

Many times, changes and proposals from the Department of Transportation came about as a result of a terrible tragedy. In 1987, a train derailed in Baltimore, Maryland, and 16 people died. The brakeman and the engineer were both under the influence of drugs at the time. Dole said people deserved to feel safe when traveling, and so she created a drug-testing program for workers in any kind of transportation industry.

Dole also paid attention to the sky. While she was secretary of transportation, a large passenger jet and a small plane crashed in midair in California, and 82 people died. People wondered if the accident could

An Amtrak derailment in Maryland in 1987 injured 170 passengers and killed 16.

have been prevented. Dole soon announced that small planes carrying more than 20 passengers had to have a warning system. The system alerted other planes in the area that the smaller plane was there. It also warned the smaller plane that it was entering busy airspace. In addition, new laws said that small planes had to be in contact with the airport when they were getting close to it.

Flight delays were another big problem for passengers. Dole wanted airlines to meet to fix their schedules so there weren't so many planes landing at the same time in major airports. Some, however, believed the problem wasn't with scheduling but instead had come about because there were too few air traffic controllers—the people at airports who communicate with the pilots.

Although the government controlled all kinds of transportation in the air and on roads, waterways, and railroad tracks, Dole didn't think that the government should be involved in every area of transportation. After all, she said, the government only had a certain amount of money for all of its programs. While she was secretary of transportation, she was in charge of the sale of a government-owned railroad, Conrail, and two government-owned airports in Washington, D.C.—Washington National Airport and Dulles International Airport. Dole said they would be managed better by private industry.

Dole's proposals and programs helped solve some existing problems. She also saw new laws passed that made transportation safer for Americans. Looking back, Dole has said making Americans safer in her role at the Department of Transportation has been one of the most rewarding parts of her career. ✑

Chapter

7 WORKING FOR THE WORKERS

⌒∽⌒

Elizabeth Dole made many improvements for the people of the United States as secretary of transportation. However, in 1987, she decided to leave Reagan's cabinet. Bob Dole wanted to run for president again, and Elizabeth wanted to go on the campaign trail with him.

Again, some criticized her and wondered why she would put her husband's goals before her own. She responded:

> *The decision was mine and mine alone, and I made the decision that was right for me ... not because I had to, but because I wanted to. And isn't that what we women have fought for all these years—the right to make our own decisions about our careers and our families?*

Elizabeth and Bob Dole walked from the White House after Elizabeth told President Reagan she was resigning from her Cabinet post.

Bob Dole dropped out of the presidential race, however, and George H.W. Bush—vice president under Ronald Reagan for eight years—won the nomination as the Republican presidential candidate. The Doles respected Bush and immediately joined his campaign for president, which he won.

As president, Bush appointed Elizabeth Dole to another Cabinet position: secretary of labor. "It didn't take me long to decide that the Department of Labor offered a wealth of opportunities to affect people's lives for the better," she said. She had experience serving in the president's Cabinet, and she was confident she could make a difference. She was sworn in on January 25, 1989.

Today there are 15 members of the Cabinet. They are departments of Agriculture, Commerce, Defense, Education, Energy, Health and Human Services, Homeland Security, Housing and Urban Development, Interior, Labor, State Transportation, the Treasury, Veterans Affairs, and Attorny General. There are also six positions with Cabinet-level rank.

The Department of Labor made decisions about the working men and women of the United States. It helped employers with their staff, and it made sure employees were working in safe, fair environments. The department also helped retired people at the end of their careers.

While secretary of labor, Dole focused her energies on young people. She wanted them to have good training so they could get good jobs. By expanding the Job Training Partnership Act of 1983, which was designed to improve the employment status of underprivileged young adults, she also found ways for young people in poorer communities to get training in the skills they needed. Sometimes companies hired children to do the work of adults. This was against the law and conditions were often unsafe. Part of Dole's job was to protect children from illegal work conditions.

George H.W. Bush (left) met with a participant from the Job Training Partnership Act and Elizabeth Dole in 1989.

Although women and minorities made up half of the working people in the United States at that time, they held less than 10 percent of the positions of leadership in companies and businesses. This came to be called the "glass ceiling"—meaning that women and minorities climbed up the business ladder, but then it seemed as if they hit a ceiling. The ceiling was clear, and they could see through it to the positions above them, but they were not allowed to go any farther. Dole made it one of her goals to allow people to break through this glass ceiling. She said:

> My objective as Secretary of Labor is to look through the "glass ceiling" to see who is on the other side, and to serve as a catalyst [means] for change.

Dole conducted many studies to find ways to solve this problem. Bob Dole supported her effort to make the workplace more equal. In the Senate, he sponsored the creation of a National Commission on the Glass Ceiling.

Elizabeth Dole's ability to help workers was not just limited to the United States. In 1989, Bob and Elizabeth Dole traveled to Poland, where democracy had just taken hold. There they met with Poland's future president and helped create a training center for workers. American carpenters, electricians, plumbers, and others traveled to Poland to help train the Polish people to build the many houses they desperately needed.

Another one of Elizabeth Dole's jobs was to help groups discuss their disagreements. In southwestern Virginia, the United Mine Workers union and the Pittston Company were locked in a bitter battle. The union was organized to protect the rights of miners, and the workers were not happy. Pittston had cut some of the programs that benefited workers. Employees refused to work, and went on strike on April 5, 1989.

Coal miners and state police faced off during the United Mine Workers strike.

The strike lasted several months. Though both sides wanted the strike to end, union leaders and Pittston managers could not come to an agreement. In October, Dole was called in to help. She recalled:

Dole, flanked by Pittston chairman Paul Douglas (left) and UMW president Richard Trumka, announced the end of the strike.

> *I saw a community torn apart, and met with families who had one member walking the picket lines, and another*

in management. In that tense atmosphere, many feared that widespread violence was unavoidable.

As secretary of labor, Dole needed to make sure both sides were happy. But the leaders for both sides had to come up with an agreement on their own—she was just there to help. She talked with leaders of the company and the union and helped them find ways to cooperate. Finally, after a long struggle and many long meetings— one lasting almost 100 hours—they agreed on a plan. Dole had done her job.

Elizabeth Dole served as secretary of labor for almost two years. On October 24, 1990, she resigned as the highest-ranking female member of the Bush administration. This time, she was not leaving her job to help her husband run for public office. She was making a career move of her own. ✍

Labor unions are designed to make sure workers are being treated fairly and that conditions for the workers are always safe. The labor movement was formally recognized by the U.S. government in the 1930s. Before that, workers had few rights. Employers could keep wages low and demand long hours. As a group, the workers had more power. They could go on strike, or refuse to work, if they thought they were being treated unfairly.

American Red Cross

800-842-2200

8 RELIEF FROM DISASTER

Chapter

❧⌘❧

On February 1, 1991, Elizabeth Dole started a new career as president of the American Red Cross. The Red Cross was formed in Switzerland by a man named Jean Henri Dunant in 1863. It was started to help people who were injured or suffering during times of war. It expanded to also help people during times of peace.

Clara Barton founded the American Red Cross in the United States in 1881 and served as its first president. She was a schoolteacher until she moved to Washington, D.C., to work for the U.S. government. During the Civil War, she had worked as a nurse and brought the troops medicine and food. She came to be called the "Angel of the Battlefield." On a visit to Europe, Barton learned about the International

Elizabeth Dole was the second woman, after founder Clara Barton, to serve the American Red Cross.

Clara Barton (1821–1912) ran the Red Cross until 1904, when she was 84.

Red Cross. When she returned, she urged the United States to join and then started the American Red Cross.

Elizabeth Dole worked at the organization's headquarters in Washington, D.C., and was in charge of more than 30,000 employees and more than a million volunteers. Here, she tried to find ways to bring such a large organization together. She said:

> You need to bring the barriers down, get people out of silos or stovepipes so that they are coordinated. Working together makes you much more efficient, and

you'll save a lot of dollars in the process.

During her first year, Dole refused to accept the $200,000 annual salary. She wanted to show employees and volunteers that she was committed and devoted to the job. If so many volunteers could give up their time to help others in need, she could give up something as well.

Dole's mother, Mary Hanford, had once worked for the Red Cross as a volunteer during World War II. She told Elizabeth that nothing had ever made her feel as important as when she was helping others through the Red Cross. Elizabeth, too, wanted to do something important, and by becoming the president of the Red Cross, she could serve and help many people.

The flag of the American Red Cross is a red cross on a white background. Many other nations in the International Red Cross also have this flag. The Red Cross flag is based on the Swiss flag, which is a white cross on a red background. In Muslim countries, the organization is called the Red Crescent Society, and their flag has a red crescent on a white background. In Israel, the flag is a red Star of David on a white background, and the organization is called the Magen David Adom.

Dole liked the organization's main mission: to take care of people during times of disaster. Today the Red Cross responds to more than 70,000 disasters every year. When hurricanes, tornadoes, floods, and wildfires destroy homes and towns, the Red Cross acts. "While many people evacuate from impending storms," Dole said, "the Red Cross does just the opposite—we move in."

Dole often went right to the site of a disaster and helped out. She filled sandbags to hold back floodwaters, handed out clothing and food, and set up temporary shelters. She went to Florida in 1992, after Hurricane Andrew destroyed homes and towns. She and many volunteers helped out at about 230 shelters the Red Cross set up.

The Red Cross provided housing to 1,300 people who became homeless after Hurricane Andrew hit in 1992.

Dole's work with the American Red Cross took her all over the world. Not all the disasters she responded to were caused by nature. The Red Cross often helped victims on both sides of a war— always remaining politically neutral. In 1991, Dole

went to Africa to help Rwandan refugees who had been forced from their homes in times of war. In 1999, during a visit to Macedonia, she saw families torn from their homes and in despair from the fighting going on there.

Dole was greatly saddened by the unfortunate human circumstances that often surrounded her in her job. She would see helpless children, and all she could do was try to give them hope for the future. She also witnessed death caused by war and disease. She felt that no one should have to suffer in these ways. She saw things that she said would haunt her for the rest of her life.

Many women have contributed to the success of the American Red Cross. In 2002, the organization hired another woman president—Marsha J. Evans. She came to the Red Cross after an almost-30-year career in the U.S. Navy. She also held a high-ranking position in the Girl Scouts of America, where she urged girls to take on community service projects.

Another major mission of the American Red Cross is to keep a supply of blood, which is used in hospitals and at disaster sites for people who have been injured and lost too much blood. The Red Cross sponsors blood drives all over the United States, where it collects blood and then tests it for diseases. The blood has to be disease-free before it can be used.

One of Dole's major contributions to the Red Cross was to improve the way the organization collected, tested, and kept track of its blood supply.

The orphans of the war in Rwanda inspired Dole to do more for the Red Cross.

She could see they needed to move into a new era. She replaced old systems with new computers and started new testing laboratories with the most updated equipment.

The $2 billion budget to run the Red Cross did not come from the government. It came from donations from people and organizations. Dole was good at raising money, but it was more than just a business to her. She said it was a job that filled her with a sense of mission like she had never known before.

To raise enough money to run the organization, she traveled around the country making speeches.

She once said:

> *As president of the American Red Cross, I barnstormed the country, asking Americans for three important personal resources: their time, their money, and, yes, their blood.*

The public always responded in times of need. Dole experienced it directly:

> *It was as president of the American Red Cross where I was privileged to see first-hand the remarkable strength of what I called America's "inner resources"—the character and compassion and generosity of the American people who donate to the Red Cross and to countless other worthy causes.*

Chapter

9 FIRST LADY OR MADAM PRESIDENT?

⟨◦✂◦⟩

Elizabeth Dole's days in politics were not over. Bob Dole decided he wanted to run for president again, and Elizabeth took a leave of absence from her job as president of the Red Cross to join her husband in his campaign. The National Republican Convention was held in San Diego, California, in August 1996. Thousands of people crowded into the convention, cheering and waving flags and banners. Hundreds of reporters and television cameras were there to record the many speeches given in support of the candidates.

Elizabeth Dole was an active participant at the convention. If people didn't already know it, they soon discovered that she was a talented speaker. Most of the speakers stood behind a podium as they

Elizabeth Dole spoke on behalf of her husband at the Republican National Convention in 1996.

spoke to the enthusiastic crowd. But Elizabeth did the opposite—she walked off the stage and strolled among the audience.

Some of her assistants told her this wouldn't work. They thought the crowd would be too loud and no one would hear her. They also worried about her walking down the stairs from the stage to the convention floor while talking and wearing high heels. But Elizabeth wasn't worried. She had a lot of experience giving speeches, and she knew it would work. The crowd was silent when she began to speak:

> *Now, you know tradition is that speakers at the Republican National Convention remain at this very imposing podium. But, tonight I'd like to break with tradition. For two reasons. One, I'm going to be speaking to friends and secondly I'm going to be speaking about the man I love and it's just a lot more comfortable for me to do that down here with you.*

She walked down the stairs and started telling stories about her husband—about his kindness, humor, and leadership. By coming down to talk among the audience, the speech seemed personal in a style that appealed to the convention attendees and to people watching on television. Some said that watching Elizabeth Dole was like watching a talk-show host.

She continued to use this personal style of speaking, and soon reporters gave it a name: the Dole Stroll. She said:

> *The warm response from those in the hall and from the commentators left me with no doubt that the best way to communicate is to speak from the heart.*

After four days of the convention, it was time for the Republican Party to formally present its presidential candidate—Bob Dole—and his running mate, Jack Kemp. They had won the Republican nomination. The 1996 election would be a hard-fought

Bob Dole (right) and Jack Kemp would run against Democratic candidates Bill Clinton and Al Gore, and Reform Party candidates H. Ross Perot and Pat Choate.

contest between Dole and Democrat Bill Clinton, who was running for a second term as president.

During her convention speech and those that followed, Elizabeth seemed like candidates' wives of the past, whose sole purpose was to support their husbands. But she promised to be a nontraditional first lady if her husband were elected. She planned to return to her job as president of the Red Cross, which would make her the first president's wife to hold a full-time job. No other first lady had ever done this. Elizabeth put it this way:

> *I knew that every First Lady in American history had been closely scrutinized by the public and the media. Each has placed her own personal imprimatur [mark of distinction] on the role of First Lady, a position for which there is no job description. Rather it reflects the personal and life experiences of each individual. Not one, however, had done what I proposed to do—hold a full-time paying job while serving as First Lady.*

Dole felt the dual roles of first lady and president of the Red Cross fit well together. The goal of both positions was to serve the public. As first lady, she planned to start a "Give Five" campaign. She would urge Americans to donate 5 percent of their time as volunteers in their communities to help others and

5 percent of their yearly income to charities.

America was already used to a nontraditional first lady. Hillary Rodham Clinton, who had been in the White House for four years, had much in common with Elizabeth Dole. Clinton was also a lawyer and dealt with issues of women's rights, children's rights, and education. The media often compared the two women's ideas, and some people even wanted a debate between Elizabeth and Hillary. But that never happened.

Elizabeth was an important part of her husband's campaign. They traveled the country, often separately, giving speeches and listening to the views and concerns of the public. Sometimes they appeared together. At other times they were speaking on opposite sides of the country. They often checked in

Like Elizabeth Dole, Hillary Rodham Clinton gave a speech at her party's convention in support of her husband.

with each other by phone or faxed each other their schedules so they would always know where the other one was going to be. Sometimes Elizabeth gave as many as 30 campaign speeches in one week.

Voters—especially women voters—liked Elizabeth Dole. They liked the idea that such an intelligent, experienced woman might be the first lady. People called Bob and Elizabeth Dole a power couple. If Bob were elected, many people believed they would both bring government experience and strong political opinions to the White House.

But Bob Dole did not win the 1996 election. Bill Clinton was elected president for a second term. Some people who had noticed Elizabeth's strengths and talents during the campaign wondered if the right Dole had been running for president.

Elizabeth returned to her job at the Red Cross and continued serving in that position until early 1999. It didn't take long for people to discover what she planned to do next. A few months later, on March 10, she made an important announcement. The morning news reported:

> *Elizabeth Dole is all but off and running for the White House, with the hope of becoming America's first female president.*

She had decided to enter the race for the

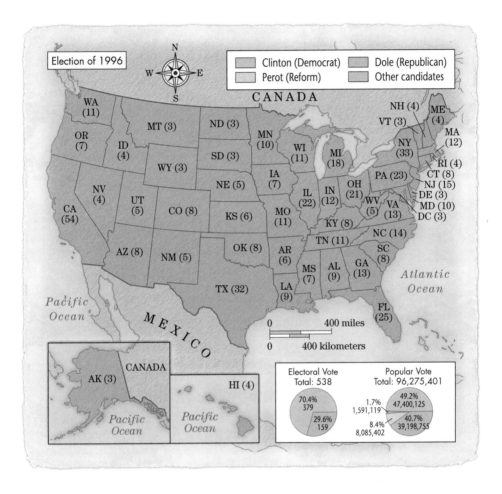

Election of 1996

Clinton (Democrat)   Dole (Republican)
Perot (Reform)   Other candidates

CANADA

WA (11)
OR (7)
ID (4)
MT (3)
ND (3)
MN (10)
WI (11)
MI (18)
NH (4)
VT (3)
ME (4)
NY (33)
MA (12)
RI (4)
CT (8)
NJ (15)
PA (23)
NV (4)
UT (5)
WY (3)
SD (3)
IA (7)
IL (22)
IN (12)
OH (21)
WV (5)
VA (13)
DE (3)
MD (10)
DC (3)
CA (54)
CO (8)
NE (5)
KS (6)
MO (11)
KY (8)
TN (11)
NC (14)
AZ (8)
NM (5)
OK (8)
AR (6)
MS (7)
AL (9)
GA (13)
SC (8)
TX (32)
LA (9)
FL (25)

Pacific Ocean
Atlantic Ocean

MEXICO

0   400 miles
0   400 kilometers

CANADA
AK (3)
Pacific Ocean
HI (4)
Pacific Ocean

Electoral Vote Total: 538
70.4% 379
29.6% 159

Popular Vote Total: 96,275,401
49.2% 47,400,125
1.7% 1,591,119
40.7% 39,198,755
8.4% 8,085,402

Republican presidential nomination in the 2000 election. People thought she had a good chance among the eight Republican candidates. Almost everyone knew this woman who had served in the Reagan and Bush Cabinets, led the Red Cross, and campaigned for her husband. The people of her hometown of Salisbury, North Carolina, urged her on. Their banners read "Run Liddy Run." In a poll

Bill Clinton had the majority of both the electoral and popular votes during the 1996 election.

in Iowa, she was in third place after Steve Forbes, a magazine publisher, and George W. Bush, the governor of Texas and son of a former president.

Dole had a good chance of winning the Republican nomination because many people wanted a woman to be president. Women still did not hold many government positions. In Congress, only 9 percent of senators were women, and just 12 percent of representatives were women. Only 6 percent of state governors were women. Many thought Dole would get lots of votes, especially from women voters.

Cindy Williams, Elizabeth's former aide, said that there was nothing better for American women than to have Dole run for president. A banner hanging at her campaign headquarters read: "Let's Make History." But Elizabeth made it clear that she didn't want people to vote for her just to have a woman president. She wanted people to vote for her because she was the best candidate to serve the country.

In her campaign speeches, she outlined her hopes for America. When she spoke at a Christian Coalition Conference, she said:

> *Ladies and gentlemen, I am running for president because I believe that we can expand economic growth and opportunity for every American. And at the same time, have a rebirth and reaffirmation of those basic principles, those unique*

values that make us America—honesty, integrity, personal responsibility, civility, and respect for one's fellow man.

In her 2000 campaign, one of Dole's goals was to get young people interested in voting.

Presidential candidates are looked at very closely by the public and the media. While Dole had many strengths, she was also criticized for what some said were weaknesses. She had been in government for decades but had never been elected to an office, they argued. She was very good at speeches she had prepared and rehearsed, and her Southern manner charmed audiences. But people wondered how she would perform at interviews when she might have to give quick, unprepared answers. They found it hard to know what her opinions were on the tougher issues.

In October 1999, Elizabeth Dole withdrew from the presidential race. Newscaster Dan Rather made this announcement: "A historic try for the White House is over. Elizabeth Dole gives up her quest to become America's first woman president." Elizabeth Dole said she quit the race because the campaign was costing too much money. Presidential campaigns usually cost about $25 million or more, and the candidates have to raise the money. Dole was a good fund-raiser, but she could not raise enough to continue to run.

Dole endorsed future president George W. Bush in the 2000 election.

Even though she dropped out of the race, Dole was praised for her attempt to make history as the first female president. Even her competition had lots of respect for her. George W. Bush called her a trailblazer and said she had been an inspiration to many women.

It was Dole's hope that someday a woman would make it to the White House as president, even if she were not the one. At 63 years old, she didn't plan on running again. But she added this encouragement to all women after she withdrew from the race:

> It's almost as if you can see some women sit up a little straighter because you're trying to empower them to understand that they can do it, they can really make a difference.

She hoped she had laid the groundwork for all women. Perhaps someday a woman would follow in her path and become president of the United States. ॐ

After Elizabeth Dole dropped out of the 2000 presidential race, George W. Bush went on to win the Republican nomination and the presidency. The 2000 election was one of the closest and most controversial presidential elections. Although Bush had the majority of electoral votes, his competition, Vice President and Democrat Al Gore, had the popular vote. The race was a close one, and the winner needed to win the electoral votes in the state of Florida. Court cases were held, citing controversial ballot counting practices in Florida during the election. Finally, Bush was counted the winner by 537 votes. He was re-elected in 2004, with similar controversy regarding ballot counting irregularity.

10 Serving Her Home State

~~~

When Elizabeth Dole's mother talked to her daughter on the phone, she often ended the conversation by saying, "Don't forget the way home." Going home is what Dole decided to do. In 2001, she and Bob moved to Salisbury, North Carolina, Dole's hometown. That year her mother celebrated her 100th birthday. Dole wanted to live close to her elderly mother, and now she could do that. She also had time to travel with her husband and get a puppy.

Many people retire around the age of 65, but Dole was not ready for retirement. "I'm mission-driven. Public service is where my passion is," she said. But she didn't know what that mission would be. She wasn't sure she wanted another government job, even though many thought she would make an

Although Elizabeth Dole spent more than three decades living in Washington, D.C., she always considered North Carolina home.

excellent vice presidential candidate. At that time, she was helping people in need in her work with Project Roundhouse, a group that helps build low-cost housing for people who lose their homes in earthquakes and hurricanes in Central America.

But soon Dole would find her mission. Republican Senator Jesse Helms of North Carolina announced his retirement in 2002, after serving his state as a senator for 30 years. Dole wanted his seat in the U.S. Senate and decided to run for office. Her main opponent was Democrat Erskine Bowles, former White House chief of staff for President Clinton. If Dole won the election, she would join the 13 other women already in the U.S. Senate. Before 2001, the most common way for a woman to become a U.S. senator was a death or resignation of a husband or father who had previously held the seat. But in 2000, three women senators were elected, and now more women have become senators by winning in their own right election.

During one of her favorite inspirational speeches, Dole said, "Well, I consider myself to be the most optimistic woman in America. I believe in our country. I believe in the innate goodness of the American people. I believe in the values that made this country what it is: courage, perseverance, generosity, faith, and a commitment to service."

Bowles had lived in North Carolina much longer than Dole, but Dole was a very popular person in her state. Dole also got support from the

Erskine Bowles became involved in politics during the 1992 election. He served as Bill Clinton's chief of staff and headed the Small Business Administration.

president of the United States. George W. Bush said in a speech:

> *You know, the thing I love about Elizabeth is she's constantly breaking what they call the glass ceiling. She shows what is possible. ... In Washington, we've got a lot of good talkers, but we need doers, people who can get the job done. And Elizabeth Dole is that kind of person.*

Bob Dole supported her as well. He had retired as senator from Kansas when he ran for president in 1996. Now he spent his time campaigning for his wife. He traveled to nearly all of North Carolina's 100 counties encouraging citizens to vote for Elizabeth.

Dole spoke to cheering supporters at her campaign headquarters in Salisbury, North Carolina, after being declared the winner.

Election Day was November 5, 2002. When the votes were in, Elizabeth had won more than half of them. She won the election. She exclaimed, "Oh, wow. What a night!" She thanked her husband, her

staff in Salisbury, and the state of North Carolina. She thanked the hundreds of volunteers and thousands of supporters who had cheered her on at rallies.

In January 2003, Dole took her oath of office and became the first woman to represent North Carolina in the U.S. Senate. Since her election, she has focused on helping the people of her state and her country. The issue of hunger especially means a lot to her. "Most definitely in our lifetime, we can certainly eliminate hunger in America," she says.

During her long career in government, Dole has held important and sometimes powerful positions. In 2005, she was elected as the first woman chair of the National Republican Senatorial Committee, which works to elect Republicans to the Senate. She and her committee came under fire, though, after the Republicans lost control of the Senate in the 2006 elections. She did not seek re-election to the committee's top spot. In addition, Dole faces a tough Senate re-election challenge in 2008.

Dole has proved, however, that women can have a place in government, and she has become a role model for women who want choices and careers. She did not lay out a blueprint for her life. "It just kind of came together as I moved along," she said. She found what she cared about, and that led her on the path of service. She gives this same advice to others:

Dole won
54 percent of
the votes to
become the 33rd
woman to
serve in the
U.S. Senate.

Find what you feel passionately about, and if it is from the heart, you're going to put in those long hours and that effort because you care. It will drive you forward, and doors are going to open up.

Elizabeth Dole has used her public service positions to help many people throughout the nation and the world. She believes the future of the United States is in its young people and their hard work. "Study hard and get good grades, because everything builds on that foundation," she advises young people. And then turning to ways to help in the community "literally does open up that whole world of volunteerism and the joy of seeing that you've made a difference for others."

She has served on the board of both of her former colleges—Duke and Harvard. Sometimes she is asked to give speeches to graduating classes. She speaks from behind a podium, but still often walks among the audiences to share her hopes for America's youth. She wants them to find a mission in life, something they care about, whether they are a volunteer, a businessperson, or a parent. She told the 2000 graduating class at Duke University:

> *You take from this ceremony much more than a diploma. You take with you the responsibility for writing the next chapter of the American story. What we become as a nation will depend in large measure on what you become—and what you believe.*

Elizabeth Dole is an example of what she encouraged these Duke graduates to become. She, too, has written a part of the American story, and her place in history isn't over yet. She hopes to continue to work to improve the lives of millions of Americans and people around the world. ℘

Life and Times

DOLE'S LIFE

1958
Graduates from Duke University with a bachelor's degree in political science

1936
Born July 29 in Salisbury, North Carolina

1960
Graduates from Harvard University with a master's degree in education and government

1940

1939
German troops invade Poland; Britain and France declare war on Germany; World War II (1939–1945) begins

1955
Rosa Parks' refusal to give up her seat on a bus to a white man inspires the civil rights movement

1959
Fidel Castro becomes leader of Cuba

WORLD EVENTS

1965

Graduates from
Harvard Law School

1966

Works at the U.S.
Department of
Health, Education,
and Welfare as staff
assistant

1968

Works for Committee
on Consumer Interests
(later called the
White House Office of
Consumer Affairs)

1965

1965

Soviet cosmonaut
Alexei Leonov
becomes the first
person to walk
in space

1966

The National
Organization for
Women (NOW) is
established to work
for equality between
women and men

1968

Civil rights leader
Martin Luther King Jr.
and presidential candi-
date Robert F. Kennedy
are assassinated two
months apart

DOLE'S LIFE

1973

Appointed to the
Federal Trade
Commission

1975

Marries Bob Dole
December 6

1976

Helps with her husband's
vice-presidential campaign

1975

1973

Arab oil embargo
of shipments to
the United States,
Europe, and Japan
creates concerns
about natural
resources

1974

Scientists find that chlo-
rofluorocarbons—chemi-
cals in coolants and pro-
pellants—are damaging
Earth's ozone layer

1976

U.S. military academies
admit women

WORLD EVENTS

1979
Leaves the FTC to help her husband campaign for president

1981
Appointed head of White House Office of Public Liaison

1983
Serves as secretary of transportation

1980
1980

1980
The United States boycotts the Olympic Games in Moscow in protest of the Soviet invasion of Afghanistan

1982
Maya Lin designs the Vietnam War Memorial, commemorating Americans who died

1983
Sally Ride becomes the first American woman to travel in space

DOLE'S LIFE

1989
Appointed
secretary of labor

1991
Serves as president
of the American
Red Cross

1995
Takes leave of
absence from the
American Red
Cross to help her
husband campaign
for president

1990

1989
Chinese troops fire
on student pro-democ-
racy demonstrators in
Tiananmen Square in
Beijing, China, killing
an estimated 2,000
or more

1990
East and West
Germany unite after
45 years of separation

1994
Genocide of 500,000
to 1 million of the
minority Tutsi group
by rival Hutu people
in Rwanda

WORLD EVENTS

1999

Campaigns for the Republican presidential nomination; withdraws from the race in October

2002

Elected U.S. senator from North Carolina

2005

Elected first woman to serve as chair of the National Senatorial Committee; serves for one year

2000

1998

Work begins on the International Space Station

2001

September 11 terrorist attacks on the two World Trade Center Towers in New York City and on the Pentagon in Washington, D.C., leave thousands dead

2006

Within a day of each other, two women become the first female presidents of their countries—Ellen Johnson-Sirleaf in Liberia and Michelle Bachelet in Chile

DATE OF BIRTH: July 29, 1936

BIRTHPLACE: Salisbury, North Carolina

FATHER: John Van Hanford
(1893–1981)

MOTHER: Mary Ella Cathey
Hanford (1901–2004)

EDUCATION: Duke University,
Oxford University,
Harvard University, and
Harvard Law School

SPOUSE: Bob Dole (1923–)

DATE OF MARRIAGE: December 6, 1975

FURTHER READING

Anderson, Dale. *Elizabeth Dole*. Philadelphia: Chelsea House Publishers, 2004.

Lucas, Eileen. *Elizabeth Dole: A Leader in Washington*. Brookfield, Conn.: Millbrook Press, 1998.

Somervill, Barbara A. *Clara Barton: Founder of the American Red Cross*. Minneapolis: Compass Point Books, 2007.

Vincent, Mary *Follow the Leader: A Dog's-Eye View of Washington, D.C.* Washington, D.C.: Eastbank Publishing, 2000.

LOOK FOR MORE SIGNATURE LIVES BOOKS ABOUT THIS ERA:

George Washington Carver: *Scientist, Inventor, and Teacher*

Cesar Chavez: *Heroic Crusader for Social Change*

Amelia Earhart: *Legendary Aviator*

Thomas Alva Edison: *Great American Inventor*

Yo-Yo Ma: *Internationally Acclaimed Cellist*

Thurgood Marshall: *Civil Rights Leader and Supreme Court Justice*

Annie Oakley: *American Sharpshooter*

Will Rogers: *Cowboy, Comedian, and Commentator*

Amy Tan: *Writer and Storyteller*

Madam C.J. Walker: *Entrepreneur and Millionare*

On the Web

For more information on this topic, use FactHound.

1. Go to *www.facthound.com*
2. Type in this book ID: 0756515831
3. Click on the *Fetch It* button.

FactHound will find the best Web sites for you.

Historic Sites

The White House
1600 Pennsylvania Avenue N.W.
Washington, DC 20500
Where the president of the United States lives and works.

The United States Capitol
Constitution Avenue and First Street N.W.
Washington, DC 20002
Where the U.S. Senate and U.S. House of Representatives meet to make and pass laws

consumer
one who buys goods and services

political party
group of people with the same ideas about government

political science
the study of government in history and the present

poll
to count votes; to make a survey

public service
a service performed for the benefit of the public; employment within a governmental system

union
organized groups of workers who try to improve working conditions and pay

Chapter 1

Page 11, line 9: Elizabeth Hanford Dole. *Hearts Touched With Fire: My 500 Favorite Inspirational Quotations*. New York: Caroll & Graf Pub., 2004, p. 162.

Page 12, line 6: Kay Bailey Hutchinson. *American Heroines: The Spirited Women Who Shaped Our Country*. New York: William Morrow, 2004, p. 120.

Page 12, line 23: Bob and Elizabeth Dole. *Unlimited Partners: Our American Story*. New York: Simon and Schuster, 1996, p. 154.

Chapter 2

Page 16, line 10: Elizabeth Dole. Phone interview. 9 March 2007.

Page 17, line 5: Rita Beamish. "Elizabeth Dole, Madam President?" *Biography*. November 1999, p. 87.

Page 19, line 11: *Unlimited Partners*, p. 51.

Page 19, line 26: Elizabeth Dole. Phone interview. 9 March 2007.

Page 21, line 16: "Nation: Liddy Makes Perfect While Looking to Move to the White House." *Time*. 1 July 1996.

Page 21, line 19: Elizabeth Dole. Phone interview. 9 March 2007.

Chapter 3

Page 23, line 11: *Hearts Touched With Fire*, p. 1.

Page 25, line 3: "Elizabeth Dole." *Duke University: The Chronicle, 2005*. 10 April 2007. http://baldwinscholars.duke.edu/featured_women/elizabeth_dole. html

Page 26, line 21: "Special Science Report." *Newsweek*. 7 March 1960. 14 April 2007. www.writing.upenn.edu/~afilreis/50s/newsweek-on-women.html

Page 32, line 18: *Elizabeth Dole, Madam President?* p. 87.

Chapter 4

Page 37, caption: "History and Tours: Past Presidents: Lyndon B. Johnson." The White House. 2 April 2007. www.whitehouse.gov/history/presidents/lj36.html

Page 39, line 13: Elizabeth Dole. Phone interview. 9 March 2007.

Page 40, line 2: *Unlimited Partners*, p. 145.

Page 43, line 11: Ibid., p. 231.

Page 45, line 6: Ibid., p. 134.

Chapter 5

Page 48, line 12: Ibid., p. 171.

Page 50, line 7: *Elizabeth Dole, Madam President?* p. 87.

Chapter 6

Page 54, sidebar: "Mission and History." U.S. Department of Transportation. 5 April 2007. www.dot.gov/mission.htm

Page 54, line 2: Elizabeth Dole. Phone interview. 9 March 2007.

Page 54, line 15: Ibid.

Chapter 7

Page 61, line 10: Nichola Gutgold. "Managing Rhetorical Roles: Elizabeth Hanford Dole from Spouse to Candidate 1996–1999." *Women and Languages*,

Spring 2001.

Page 62, line 9: *Unlimited Partners*, p. 272–273.

Page 64, line 12: National Women's Hall of Fame. *Women of the Hall.* www.greatwomen.org.

Page 66, line 5: *Unlimited Partners*, p. 280.

Chapter 8

Page 70, line 9: Elizabeth Dole. Phone interview. 9 March 2007.

Page 71, line 27: *Unlimited Partners*, p. 309.

Page 75, line 2: *Hearts Touched with Fire*, p. 4.

Page 75, line 9: Ibid., p. 91.

Chapter 9

Page 78, line 12: Elizabeth Dole's GOP Convention Speech. 14 Aug. 1996. www.pbs.org/newshour/convention96/floor_speeches/elizabeth_dole.html

Page 79, line 4: *Hearts Touched With Fire*, pp. 6–7.

Page 80, line 12: *Unlimited Partners*, p. 15.

Page 82, line 23: Jane Robelot. "Is America Ready for a Woman President?" *CBS This Morning*, 11 March 1999.

Page 84, line 23: Elizabeth Dole. "Presidential Candidate Elizabeth Dole Delivers Remarks at Christian Coalition Conference." Washington Transcript Service. 1 Oct. 1999.

Page 86, line 5: Dan Rather, Phil Jones, and Bob Schieffer. "Elizabeth Dole Succumbs to Big Money." *CBS Evening News with Dan Rather*. 20 Oct. 1999.

Page 87, line 17: Ibid.

Chapter 10

Page 89, line 3: *Hearts Touched With Fire*, p. 61.

Page 89, line 11: Chris Black. "Elizabeth Dole Still Perfectly Driven." *National Journal*. 16 June 2001.

Page 90, sidebar: *Hearts Touched With Fire*, pp. 8–9.

Page 91, line 3: George W. Bush. "Remarks at a Dinner for Senatorial Candidate Elizabeth Dole in Greensboro, North Carolina." *Weekly Compilation of Presidential Documents*. 25 July 2002.

Page 92, line 8: Elizabeth Dole. "Senatorial Candidate Elizabeth Dole (R-NC) Delivers Remarks." Washington Transcript Service. 5 Nov. 2002.

Page 92, line 8: Elizabeth Dole. Phone interview. 9 March 2007.

Page 93, line 7: Ibid.

Page 93, line 24: Ibid.

Page 94, line 1: Duke 2000 Commencement Address. Duke University: Baldwin Scholars. http://baldwinscholars.duke.edu/featured_women/elizabeth_dole.html

Page 95, line 15: Ibid.

Beamish, Rita. "Elizabeth Dole, Madam President?" *Biography*, November 1999.

Black, Chris. "Elizabeth Dole Still Perfectly Driven." *National Journal*. 16 June 2001.

Bush, George W. "Remarks at a Dinner for Senatorial Candidate Elizabeth Dole in Greensboro, North Carolina." *Weekly Compilation of Presidential Documents*. 25 July 2002.

Dole, Bob, and Elizabeth Dole. *Unlimited Partners: Our American Story*. New York: Simon and Schuster, 1996.

Dole, Elizabeth Hanford. *Hearts Touched with Fire: My 500 Favorite Inspirational Quotations*. New York: Caroll & Graf Pub., 2004.

Dole, Elizabeth. "Presidential Candidate Elizabeth Dole Delivers Remarks at Christian Coalition Conference." *Washington Transcript Service* 1 Oct. 1999.

Dole, Elizabeth. "Senatorial Candidate Elizabeth Dole (R-NC) Delivers Remarks." Washington Transcript Service. 5 Nov. 2002.

Gutgold, Nichola. "Managing Rhetorical Roles: Elizabeth Hanford Dole from Spouse to Candidate 1996–1999." *Women and Language*. Spring, 2001.

Harper, Jennifer. "Is America Ready for Madame President?" *Insight on the News*. 28 Dec. 1998.

Hutchison, Kay Bailey. *American Heroines: The Spirited Women Who Shaped Our Country*. New York: William Morrow, 2004.

Kauffman, Hattie. "Elizabeth Dole Discusses Refugee Crisis." *CBS This Morning*. 2 April 1999.

"Labor: Pittston Coal Strike Resolved." *Facts on File World News Digest*. 5 Jan. 1990.

Letters. *Time*. 22 July 1996.

Lyden, Jacki. "Profile: North Carolina Senate Primary Races." National Public Radio, *All Things Considered*. 30 Aug. 2002.

"Other U.S. News: Third Brake Light for Autos Ordered." *Facts on File World News Digest*. 4 Nov. 1983.

Ramesh, Ponnuru. "The Other Dole Campaign." *National Review*. 9 Feb. 1998.

Rather, Dan, Phil Jones, and Bob Schieffer. "Elizabeth Dole Succumbs to Big Money." *CBS Evening News with Dan Rather*. 20 Oct. 1999.

Robelot, Jane. "Is America Ready for a Woman President?" *CBS This Morning*. 11 March 1999.

Shields, Mark, and Robert Novak. Interview with Elizabeth Dole. *CNN Evans*. 10 Aug. 2002.

Dana Meachen Rau is an author, editor, and illustrator of children's books. A graduate of Trinity College in Hartford, Connecticut, she has written more than 200 books for children, many of them nonfiction in subjects including astronomy, history, and geography. She has written numerous biographies as well. She lives in Burlington, Connecticut, with her husband and two children.

Image Credits

AP Photo/Rusty Burroughs, cover (top), 4–5; AP Photo/Dole Campaign, cover (bottom), 2; Ron Sachs/CNP/Corbis, 8, 13; Brooks Kraft/Corbis, 10, 14, 16, 31, 33, 44, 88, 96 (top left), 97 (top), 98 (top left); Gail Mooney/Corbis, 18; Hulton Archive/Getty Images, 20; Bernard Hoffman/Time Life Pictures/Getty Images, 22, 96 (top right); Duke University Archives, 24; Mark Kauffman/Time Life Pictures/Getty Images, 27; Ted Russell/Time Life Pictures/Getty Images, 29; Paul Conklin/Pix Inc./Time Life Pictures/Getty Images, 30; Bettmann/Corbis, 34, 40, 42, 55, 60, 66; LBJ Library photo by Frank Muto, 37; Keystone/CNP/Getty Images, 39; Dirck Halstead/Liaison/Getty Images, 46; Olivier Rebbot/Woodfin Camp/Time Life Pictures/Getty Images, 48, 98 (top right); Wally McNamee/Corbis, 50; AP Photo, 52, 99 (top); Don Johnston/Stone/Getty Images, 56; Marty Katz/Time Life Pictures/Getty Images, 58; Diana Walker/Time Life Pictures/Getty Images, 63, 100 (top left); William F. Campbell/Time Life Pictures/Getty Images, 65; AP Photo/J. Scott Applewhite, 68; Corbis/Royalty-Free, 70; Raymond Gehman/Corbis, 73; Getty Images, 74, 100 (top right); AP Photo/Bob Galbraith, 76; J. David Ake/AFP/Getty Images, 79; Najlah Feanny/Corbis, 81; Don Emmert/AFP/Getty Images, 85; Luke Frazza/AFP/Getty Images, 86; Cynthia Johnson/Time Life Pictures/Getty Images, 91; Brian Gomsak/Getty Images, 93, 101 (top); Reuters/Mike Theiler/Corbis, 94; Arnold Gold/Corbis Sygma, 95; Library of Congress, 96 (bottom, all), 97 (bottom); Photodisc, 98 (bottom); Svetlana Zhurkin, 99 (bottom); Scott Peterson/Liaison/Getty Images, 100 (bottom); Digital Vision, 101 (bottom).